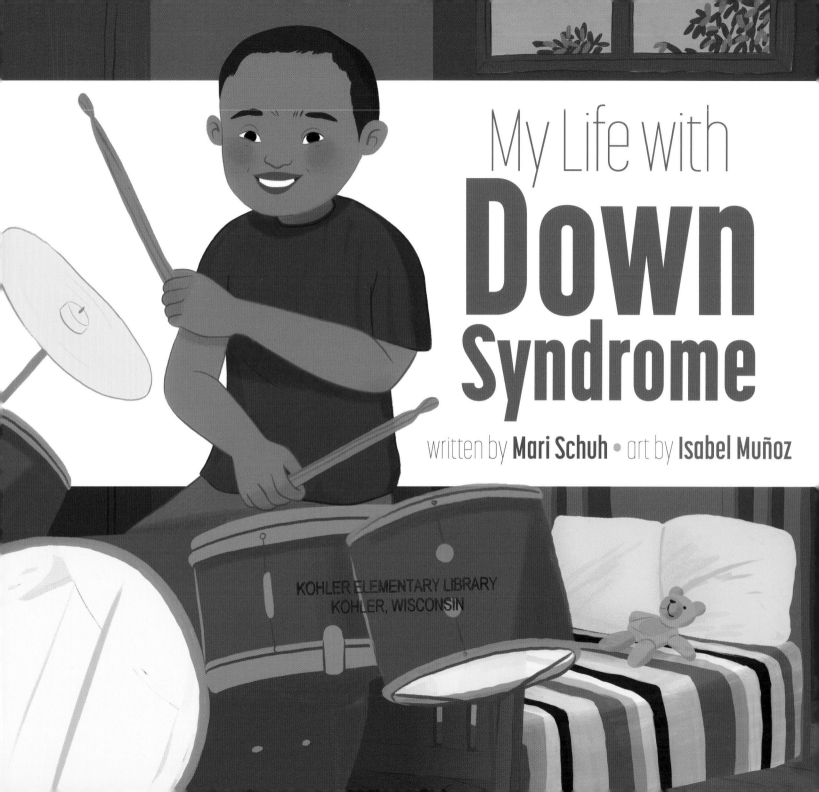

My Life with
Down
Syndrome

written by **Mari Schuh** • art by **Isabel Muñoz**

AMICUS ILLUSTRATED and AMICUS INK
are published by Amicus
P.O. Box 1329, Mankato, MN 56002
www.amicuspublishing.us

Editor: Gillia Olson
Designer: Kathleen Petelinsek

Library of Congress Cataloging-in-Publication Data
Names: Schuh, Mari C., 1975- author. | Muñoz, Isabel, illustrator.
Title: My life with Down syndrome / Mari Schuh ; illustrated by Isabel Muñoz.
Description: Mankato, Minnesota : Amicus, [2021] | Series: My life with... | Includes bibliographical references. | Audience: Ages 6-9 |
Audience: Grades 2-3 | Summary: "Meet Peter! He loves the drums and gym. He also has Down Syndrome. Peter is real and so are his
experiences. Learn about his life in this illustrated narrative nonfiction picture book for elementary students"—Provided by publisher.
Identifiers: LCCN 2019047369 (print) | LCCN 2019047370 (ebook) | ISBN 9781681519937 (library
binding) | ISBN 9781681526409 (paperback) | ISBN 9781645490784 (pdf)
Subjects: LCSH: Children with Down syndrome—United States—Biography—Juvenile literature. | Down syndrom—Juvenile literature.
Classification: LCC HV897.W6 S38 2021 (print) | LCC HV897.W6 (ebook) | DDC 616.85/88420092 [B]—dc23
LC record available at https://lccn.loc.gov/2019047369
LC ebook record available at https://lccn.loc.gov/2019047370

Printed in the United States of America

HC 10 9 8 7 6 5 4 3 2 1
PB 10 9 8 7 6 5 4 3 2 1

For Peter, Greta, and Kellen-MS

About the Author

Mari Schuh's love of reading began with cereal boxes at
the kitchen table. Today, she is the author of hundreds of
nonfiction books for beginning readers. With each book, Mari
hopes she's helping kids learn a little bit more about the world
around them. Find out more about her at marischuh.com.

About the Illustrator

To paint for a living was Isabel Muñoz' dream, and now she's
proud to be the illustrator of several children books. Isabel
works from a studio based in a tiny, cloudy, green and lovely
town in the north of Spain. You can follow her at isabelmg.com.

Hi! I'm Peter. I love music! I play the drums.
Bom, bom, bom. I've been playing since I was really
little. I also have Down syndrome. It's OK. Everyone is
different in some way. Let me tell you about my life.

Kids who have Down syndrome are born with it. We have an extra chromosome. It affects how we learn and how we look. My eyes are a bit small and slanted. I have small ears. Sometimes my tongue hangs out. My face and nose might look flatter than yours.

Down syndrome usually causes health problems. Tubes inside our ears can be narrow. Germs can get trapped and cause ear infections a lot. We also don't see as well as other kids. My friend Zoe has to wear glasses.

About half of kids with Down syndrome
have heart problems. I had heart surgery
when I was younger. I'm pretty healthy now.

I go to the same school as my brothers and sisters. I like the routine of my school days. I know what to do. I always sit on the same seat on the school bus. That's my spot!

I can get upset when I have to quickly change what I'm doing. I never want gym class to end. I want to keep playing! A teacher's helper is with me all day. She calms me down. She reminds me that it's time to go to my next class.

I can do lots of things, but I learn more slowly than other kids. My class is small. I learn better that way. Today, a teacher's helper works with me to learn colors, shapes, and letters.

I join other classes for band, gym, and art.
I also join them for story time and snacks.
Sometimes we have dance parties!

At school, I make new friends all the time.

But lunchtime can be hard. Sometimes I don't like the school's food. I get upset. A teacher's helper tells me it's OK. She helps me feel better.

When I get home from school,
my dog Sheldon is waiting for
me. He's one of my best pals.
We snuggle. We play fetch, too.

Some kids with Down syndrome have weak muscles. Not me. I'm strong and have lots of energy. I like to climb and play.

Ugh, it's really hot outside today. Maybe I shouldn't have played so much. I do get hot easily. Sometimes I forget that.

When I'm not playing or running around, I love to listen to music. I listen to songs on my tablet computer. I don't need any help. I know how to find my favorite songs.

Now I want to play my drums. When I'm older, I want to be in the school band. It might take me longer to learn. But I won't let that stop me.

Meet Peter

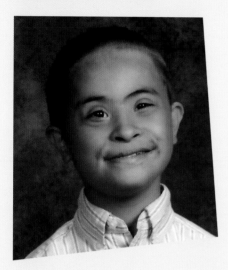

Hello! I'm Peter. I have a big family. I live with my mom, dad, three brothers, and four sisters. I am adopted. So are my four sisters and one of my brothers. But that's not all! We have three dogs and one cat. We all live in La Crosse, Wisconsin. I like to swing, ride scooters, swim, and eat. I also love to listen to music and make my own music, especially with drums.

Respecting People with Down Syndrome

Treat a person with Down syndrome like you would any person. Be friendly, respectful, and kind.

Don't stare at kids with Down syndrome. It is not polite.

Expect kids with Down syndrome to follow rules, just like everyone else.

Play and be friends with kids who have Down syndrome, just like you would any kid.

No two people in the world are the same. Each person has things that they like and dislike. This is true for people with Down syndrome, too.

When you meet someone with Down syndrome, say hi and ask them what their name is. You might make a new friend.

Helpful Terms

chromosome A very small part of a cell that contains genes. Genes control how people look and grow. Genes are passed from parents to their children. People with Down syndrome have 47 chromosomes instead of 46.

ear infection An illness in the ear that is caused by germs or viruses. Ear infections can hurt and can cause a fever.

energy The power to do things without getting tired.

favorite Something that a person likes the best.

routine A regular way or pattern of doing things.

surgery An operation that fixes a part of the body.

Read More

Duling, Kaitlyn. **My Friend Has Down Syndrome.**
All Kinds of Friends. Minneapolis: Jump!, Inc., 2019.

Levine, Michelle. **Down Syndrome**. Living with... Mankato, Minn.: Amicus High Interest, 2015.

McAneney, Caitie. **Different but Equal: Appreciating Diversity**. Spotlight on
Social and Emotional Learning. New York: PowerKids Press, 2020.

Websites

BBC THREE: THINGS PEOPLE WITH DOWN SYNDROME ARE TIRED OF HEARING

https://www.bbc.co.uk/programmes/p043bgqp

People with Down Syndrome let you know what they are tired of hearing.

KIDS QUEST: DISABILITIES AND HEALTH

https://www.cdc.gov/ncbddd/kids/index.html

Learn more about kids who have disabilities.

UTAH DOWN SYNDROME FOUNDATION

http://www.udsf.org/

Read or watch videos about Down Syndrome.

Every effort has been made to ensure that these websites are appropriate for children. However, because of the nature of the Internet, it is impossible to guarantee that these sites will remain active indefinitely or that their contents will not be altered.